BRAVE SCOTS

ROBERT THE BRUCE

WRITTEN BY
GARY SMAILES

ILLUSTRATED BY
CRAIG HOWARTH

For Jacob, Ben & Poppy
G. Smailes

Design - Winsome Malcolm

Reprographics - GWP Graphics

Printing - Printer Trento, Italy

Published by

GW Publishing
PO Box 6091
Thatcham
Berks
RG19 8XZ

Tel +44 (0) 1635 268080

www.gwpublishing.com

ISBN 09551564-6-7
978-09551564-6-5

Robert Bruce was a Brave Scot and a king of Scotland. His life was one of war, murder and betrayal. This book tells the amazing story of a man whose destiny led him to fight against three English kings and bring freedom to Scotland. If you want to know the real story of one of the most important Brave Scots ever to live, then read on...

Robert Bruce, Robert Bruce and Robert Bruce

Robert Bruce lived in Scotland over 700 years ago. Back then, the country was a very different place. It had its own laws, its own army and even its own king. However, the king's life wasn't simple, since the size and remoteness of his kingdom made it impossible for him to rule over all of his people at once. To make his task easier the king split Scotland into smaller pieces and gave them to his favourite knights. The king told his knights just how to rule over the people living on their land. The knights then listened to the king's demands and told the people exactly what their monarch wanted them to do.

ARE YOU SURE THIS IS WHAT THE KING WANTS US TO DO?

ERR. .YES AND HE ALSO WANTED YOU TO MAKE MY LUNCH WHEN YOU HAVE FINISHED.

This might sound like a good deal but the knights didn't get the land for free. They didn't have to pay the king any money; instead they owed the king a big favour, which was probably much worse. It meant that when the king decided to start a war, the knights would be expected to turn up and fight whether they wanted to or not. As if this weren't bad enough, the knights would also be expected to bring along as many soldiers as they could afford.

Our story begins with a knight called Robert de Brus. He had come from France with William the Conqueror in 1066 and probably fought in the Battle of Hasting against King Harold. He was a good knight and was rewarded by the king of England with lots of land in England and then later in Scotland. The problem was that in medieval times the English didn't like the French very much, so when Robert de Brus died, the family changed its name to ... well ... Bruce. However, though the family had hated the name Brus, they loved the name Robert. In fact over the next three

generations they named their boys just that. There was our hero — Robert Bruce, his dad — Robert Bruce and his granddad, you've guessed it — Robert Bruce.
To keep things simple we will call them the following names:

Robert Bruce
(our hero)

Bruce, Earl of Carrick
(our hero's dad)

Bruce the Competitor
(our hero's granddad)

Got that? I hope so, because I think I am a bit confused already.

Bruce the Competitor

The first Robert Bruce that we need to worry about was our hero's granddad, Bruce the Competitor. At the time of this story, the king of Scotland was a man called Alexander II. Now, Alexander was a worried man. No matter how hard he tried, his wife couldn't give birth to a boy. This meant that if the king were to die suddenly, there would be no heir to take over the Scottish throne. This isn't a problem for normal people like you and me, but for a king it's a real headache. Alexander II came up with a cunning plan and decided to promise Bruce the Competitor that he could be the next king of Scotland. As it happened, the king was worrying for no reason. His queen, Marie de Coucy, soon became pregnant and gave birth to a baby boy.

Alexander was overjoyed, but as you can imagine Bruce the Competitor was pretty annoyed, since it meant he would never be king. In fact, the Bruce family was so annoyed that they never did forget the broken promise — even after the king was dead.

King
Alexander died
eight years after his son was
born. Now, royal families are
famous for not being very good at
thinking up names for their kids.
The king of Scotland was no
different. After much thought he
decided to call his son … Alexander.
Wow, it must have taken him all
night to think that one up! So,
when young Alexander was made
king in 1249, he became known as
King Alexander III.

Though he had the same name as
his dad, Alexander III didn't have
the same problem with kids. He
had loads! No, this king had a
different problem — all of his

children died young
and, by 1286, Alexander III had no
children left alive who could take
over the throne if he were to die
suddenly. This would have been
fine if the king had lived long
enough to have more children, but
history never works like that. It all
changed on a stormy winter's
night. The king had spent the day
at his castle in Edinburgh and that
night decided to ride home to see
his queen. A huge storm was
raging but the king refused to stop.
The road he took went close to a
huge cliff. In normal weather it was
pretty scary, but in the middle of a
huge storm it was downright

dangerous. Suddenly, a flash of lightning startled the king's horse. It panicked and threw him over the edge of the cliff. Alexander plummeted to his death on the rocky beach far below.

With Alexander dead and no children to take over the throne, Scotland was left with no king or queen. It turned out that the only member of Alexander's family left alive who could rule Scotland was his young granddaughter, Margaret. However, as is always the case with these things, there was a problem, well two problems. The first was that she was only five years old. The second was that she lived in Norway. Scotland was pretty desperate for a ruler and decided to ignore these problems. So, they told the young girl to get onto the next boat to Scotland.

Margaret might have turned out to be a very good queen. She might have united Scotland and made the country great — but we will never know. During the voyage to Scotland, disaster struck. She quickly became ill and died before even reaching the shore. Scotland was now in trouble and had no king or queen.

King John

With no king or queen, Scotland had a big problem!

The country needed a monarch to tell the knights what to do. So, desperate to find somebody, the Scottish people started looking all over the place for a suitable king. Lots of Scots (and Englishmen and Frenchmen and Danes) thought that they would make a good king, but only two people had a realistic claim to the throne — Robert the Competitor and a man called John Balliol.

By now, you know all about Robert the Competitor's claim to the throne and the dead king's promise to him.
He had never forgotten what Alexander II had said and I bet that he never stopped telling his mates that he should have been the next king of Scotland.

Yet, Alexander II's promise was not the only reason that Bruce the Competitor thought he should be king. Our hero's granddad did actually have a decent claim to the throne. You see, he was related to a long dead Scottish king called David I, who had ruled Scotland between 1124 and 1153. The problem was that John Balliol was also related to King David, and therefore thought that he should be king instead. Pretty complicated eh?

Now John and Robert both wanted to

be king really badly, so badly in fact that they were prepared to start a war with each other. With no king to rule the country and no one in Scotland who could control them and it looked as if the two Scottish knights and their armies would end up fighting. However, at the last minute Bishop Fraser of St Andrews had one of the worst ideas of his life. On the 7th October 1290, he wrote a letter to the king of England, Edward I, asking him to decide just who should be the next king of Scotland. The bishop had forgotten that King Edward was a crafty and greedy old king, who

wanted more than anything else in the world to make Scotland part of his kingdom. Now he had his chance, all thanks to the dozy bishop!

The English king, Edward I, called a great meeting at Berwick to decide if Robert Bruce or John Balliol should be the next king. On 17th November 1292, Edward made his decision and John Balliol was crowned King John of Scotland. The reason he chose John Balliol was simple — he thought he could boss him about.

The king's choice left many Scottish people very angry, including the Bruce family who were furious. In fact, they were so mad they refused to serve the new king of Scotland. This left them with a bit of a problem. They were knights and needed to serve a king. So, they decided that since they wouldn't serve John Balliol, now called King John, they would find a new master. The answer was simple; they decided to start serving the next nearest king — Edward I, king of England.

Scotland now had a new ruler, but the crafty English king still had plans for Scotland. He began to boss King John about and constantly told him how he should be ruling Scotland. This annoyed everyone, but just when it looked as though King Edward was going to get his way, it all changed. In 1294 England declared war on France. Now, King Edward really did enjoy bossing people about, but something he enjoyed even more was fighting a good war. With Frenchmen to kill, King Edward seemed to forget all about bossing King John around and left Scotland alone.

King Edward

With Edward in France, many Scottish knights saw a chance to break free from the king and thought up a plan to attack England. Though many Scottish knights didn't like England interfering with Scotland, they didn't think that starting a fight with Edward was a very good idea. After all he had one of the best armies in the world. This was how the Bruce family thought and they refused to join with the Scottish rebels. Instead, they stayed on the English side, hoping that King John would be removed from the throne and replaced with a Bruce.

King Edward had lots of spies in Scotland and soon found out all about the Scottish plans to attack England. It was clear that his days of bullying King John were over, and with the war in France coming to an end, he decided it was time to act. As we all know the English king liked a good war and when he ran out of Frenchmen to kill, he decided he would force the Scots into a fight. The cheeky king demanded that the Scots hand over some of their most important castles, knowing perfectly well that the Scots would refuse. The Scottish and English kings soon stopped being friends and even started to become enemies. So, in 1296, when a group of English merchants was killed in the Scottish town of Berwick, Edward I had the excuse he needed to start a war in Scotland.

13

King Edward now did just what he liked doing best — leading his army to war. He marched his men north and attacked Berwick. The town was not very well defended and was quickly overcome. Nasty King Edward wanted revenge for the dead merchants and ordered that all the Scots living in Berwick be murdered.

The killing lasted for three days. It was now the Scots' turn to be angry. They wanted revenge, so they formed an army and rode to find the English. The two forces finally met at Dunbar, but the battle went badly for the inexperienced Scottish warriors and they were easily beaten.

With the Scottish army out of the way, greedy King Edward was free to simply march into Scotland and take what he wanted. The Scottish king had no choice but to surrender to Edward. When they finally met, King John was forced to stand in front the English king whilst Edward ripped the Scottish coat of arms from the king of Scotland's coat. From that day,

King John was known to all as Toom Tabard, which meant empty coat. However, those who really hated John simply called him King Nobody. King John, humiliated, ran off to France to hide from the naughty English king.

King Edward now controlled Scotland, which was nice for him, but pretty horrible for the Scots.

14

Yet even as the English armies took control of the Scottish castles, one Brave Scot was not prepared to simply stand by and watch. His name was William Wallace. His father was a Scottish knight who had been killed by the English.

The mighty William Wallace not only wanted revenge for his father's death, he also wanted freedom for Scotland. He collected together a Scottish army and started to attack, slowly taking back castles and towns. William Wallace might have been fighting for revenge and freedom, but he was also fighting for King John. He made it clear to everyone that if he could win Scotland back, then he would put John back on the throne. This was great for John Balliol, but awful news for the Bruce family who still really wanted to be king. At first our hero, Robert Bruce, and

his father remained loyal to the king of England but Bruce was never happy. He couldn't stand by and watch as his fellow Scots were being killed, so he left his father and joined the Scottish side, even if it meant that King John might return as king of Scotland.

Robert Bruce and other knights gathered together their forces and prepared to meet the English in battle. Importantly, William Wallace was not part of this army. Bruce had never really liked him and he was not invited to join the fight. Instead Wallace was off fighting the English in another part of Scotland.

The battle took place at Irvine — well actually it didn't take place at Irvine. Before the fighting had even begun, some of the Scottish knights caught sight of the advancing English army and became so scared they simply surrendered. The battle was over before it had even begun and the Scots had lost. Bruce and his men escaped with their lives, but only just.

William Wallace

Next it was Wallace's turn. The English marched to find him and the two armies met on 11th September 1297, at a small wooden bridge close to Stirling Castle. The Scots fought bravely and, after a mighty battle, managed to defeat the English army. Wallace now controlled Scotland.

After the Battle of Stirling Bridge, William Wallace became more and more powerful, taking back control of most of Scotland. All this time King Edward had been fighting in France, but he knew all about Wallace and had come to hate the Brave Scot. So when the king returned to England he was furious. As we know, King Edward loved a good battle. So it shouldn't be a surprise to learn that the first thing he did when he returned to England was to gather up his army and set out for Scotland. Wallace was ready for Edward and the two great armies met just outside Falkirk. On the day, Wallace was no match for the English king. Edward was an experienced solider and had won

many battles. The Scots were beaten by the charges of the English knights and the arrows from their mighty longbows.

Though many Scottish warriors died at the Battle of Falkirk, Wallace escaped with his life and fled to France. However, by the time he returned to Scotland a few years later, things had changed. Wallace had few friends left and he was quickly captured. King Edward brought him to London and had him horribly killed. He was hanged until nearly dead, and then cut down and his insides pulled out while he was still alive. Wallace didn't die until they cut out his still-beating heart. Once dead his head was chopped off and his body cut into four parts. The head was put on a spike on London Bridge and his arms and legs sent to towns all over Scotland.

If King Edward thought that controlling Scotland would be as simple as winning just one big battle and killing their hero — he was mistaken. Though they had no army, the Scottish people still ruled their own country. King Nobody… sorry I should have said King John… had given up the Scottish throne and was now hiding in France. It was decided that two men should become the Guardians

It made sense to choose Bruce to help rule Scotland since he had a claim to the throne, but why Comyn? Well this also made sense, since Comyn's uncle was John Balliol, the exiled king of Scotland. This set-up would have been fine, apart from the small fact that Robert and John hated each other. Luckily, they loved Scotland and were prepared to work together to keep the country safe.

of Scotland — our hero, Robert Bruce, and a man called John Comyn.

Bruce's plan was simple — he wanted to be king. In fact, whenever you read or hear anything about Robert Bruce you should remember that he really, really, really wanted to be king of Scotland. This explains everything he did: whether fighting for the English or the Scots, he had just one thing on his mind — "how can I become king?"

So in 1302, when he found out about a Scottish plan to bring John Balliol back to Scotland, he had to act. If Balliol were once again placed on the Scottish throne, then Bruce's claim to be king of Scotland would be useless. No matter what happened with the English, Bruce just couldn't let Balliol become king. So Bruce had no choice but to help the English fight against the Scots and Balliol. On the 16th February, he changed sides again! Bruce wasn't a traitor and he didn't want Edward to rule Scotland, he just wanted to make sure King John stayed off the throne.

The Murder of John Comyn

King Edward was not the kind of man to give up on his plan to rule Scotland and he kept on attacking and capturing Scottish towns and castles. By 1304 the only castle left in Scottish hands was Stirling Castle, only a few miles from the site of William Wallace's famous victory over the English at Stirling Bridge. Yet even as things looked bad for the Scottish people, Robert Bruce also refused to give up on his dream, a dream to become the king of Scotland. So, whilst the king was breaking down the walls of Stirling Castle, Robert Bruce was making a secret pact with Bishop Lamberton for a new war against England and Edward, a war that would this time see him crowned as the king of Scotland.

By 1304 Scotland had been fighting against the English for years. Some men like William Wallace had stayed loyal to Scotland, refusing to bow to King Edward, but they had simply ended up murdered. However, this was not the case for our hero. He had survived, doing what he needed to do to avoid being captured and killed, all the time dreaming of becoming king. Now his time had come. However, before he could even think about fighting the English, he needed to deal with his Scottish enemies.

Though many Scottish knights were prepared to join together to fight the English, they still supported King John and wanted to see him on the throne, NOT Bruce. The biggest and strongest of these enemies was King John's nephew, John Comyn. Robert Bruce could not hope to be king whilst John Comyn was in Scotland and he needed a plan to get him out of the country. The problem is that Bruce's plan was just awful. We don't know exactly what happened, but over the years a legend has grown from the events.

It goes like this…

John Comyn and Robert Bruce met in secret. They made a pact that Comyn would help Bruce to become king, but in retun Comyn would be given all of Bruce's land. The deal was written down and sealed by dripping hot wax onto the paper. Each man pushed a specially shaped piece of metal into the cooling wax to form a unique seal. The paper was then torn in two and half given to each man.

It turned out that Comyn never really trusted Bruce, but you can't really blame him, can you? After all Bruce had fought for both sides and Comyn knew that our hero didn't want his uncle, John Balliol, to be king again. Comyn now saw his chance to get rid of Bruce once and for all. He went to King Edward and told him of Bruce's plan to become king of Scotland. The king was furious and demanded that Bruce come to his court to explain his actions.

When Bruce arrived he was shown Comyn's part of the agreement, which contained his wax seal. However, the English king liked Bruce and wanted to see proof of betrayal before he acted. So Edward told Bruce to bring his seal to the court, so that it could be compared to the wax...

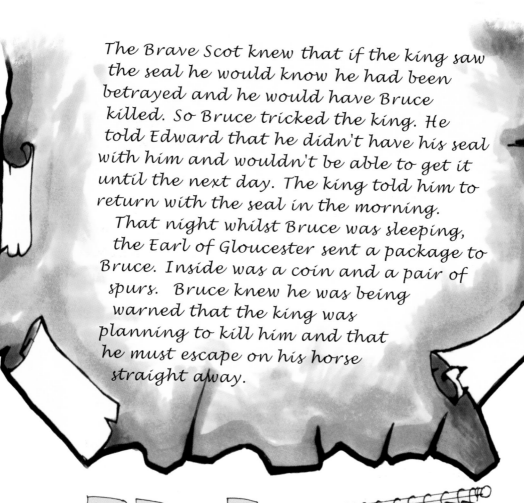

The Brave Scot knew that if the king saw the seal he would know he had been betrayed and he would have Bruce killed. So Bruce tricked the king. He told Edward that he didn't have his seal with him and wouldn't be able to get it until the next day. The king told him to return with the seal in the morning.

That night whilst Bruce was sleeping, the Earl of Gloucester sent a package to Bruce. Inside was a coin and a pair of spurs. Bruce knew he was being warned that the king was planning to kill him and that he must escape on his horse straight away.

NOT THAT KIND OF SEAL!

This is all legend and we don't know if it's true or not, but the next bit is definitely part of history...

but they soon became angry and began to argue. A vicious fight broke out. Bruce pulled out a dagger and stabbed Comyn. He slumped onto the steps of the altar in a pool of blood. Bruce's enemy died in the church. Our hero quickly escaped. Even in medieval times people knew murder was wrong, but to kill someone in a church was very bad indeed. King Edward would want his revenge.

Bruce jumped straight onto his horse and headed for Scotland to find Comyn. The two men met in front of the altar at Greyfriars church in Dumfries. They greeted each other with a kiss of friendship on the cheek. Now, no one knows what the men then talked about,

Bruce on the Run

Robert Bruce had come a long way and he wasn't going to let a little thing like the cold-blooded murder of a fellow Scot stop him from being king. So he quickly gathered up an army and set off to capture as many Scottish castles as he could manage. Bruce headed for Scone and, on 25th March 1306, had himself quickly crowned king of Scotland. With King John still alive in France and King Edward refusing to accept Bruce as king — yet another war was just around the corner.

QUICK! MAKE ME A KING BEFORE ANYONE COMES.

By now King Edward must have been getting pretty bored of fighting the Scots. So instead of going to Scotland himself, he sent a man called Aymer de Valence. Clever King Edward knew that Valence was related to the murdered John Comyn and that he hated Bruce. In fact he hated Bruce so much that he flew a special flag at the front of his army. It was shaped like a dragon and told his enemies that he would fight with no rules, take no prisoners and kill everybody he could.

The two armies met at Methven, near Perth, on 18th June 1306. Bruce expected the two armies to fight the next day, but Valence had other plans. He waited until it was dark and with the Scottish soldiers fast asleep, he attacked — not very fair really. King Robert wasn't ready and the Scottish army was easily beaten. After only three months of being crowned as the king of Scotland, Bruce was beaten in battle and was running for his life from the English soldiers. Not a very good start!

Robert Bruce was a Brave Scot and though things looked bad, he didn't give up. Instead he collected what soldiers he could find and headed west through the hills towards Loch Lomond. Now, we must remember that even though Bruce was king, not all of the powerful Scottish knights were on his side. So, when he met his enemy, John MacDougall, and his army, Bruce was forced to fight yet another battle. Surprisingly it turned out that, even though Bruce was king, he was not yet a great

commander and once again he was defeated. Lucky Bruce managed to escape once again, but this time his army was destroyed.

Bruce headed southwest towards Ireland and then he did the strangest thing... he simply disappeared.

      Puff — gone!

Well not actually... he didn't vanish in real life... he only disappeared from history. We have no records of where Robert Bruce went or what he did over the next few months, but what we do know is that he survived to fight another day.

One famous legend does survive and gives us a glimpse into what it was like for our hero on the run. It tells us the story of Bruce and the spider and goes something like this...

Whilst the Scottish king was running from the English, he found a cave in which he could hide. It was a very bad time for Bruce and things looked very black indeed. Despite his best efforts the English still ruled Scotland, his army was destroyed, his friends were captured and the powerful king of England wanted him dead. As Bruce sat in a dark cold cave thinking what to do next, his eyes noticed a small spider trying to spin a web.

Each time the spider started, the web became tangled and it had to start all over again. As Bruce watched, the spider finally managed to spin a good web. Suddenly the king knew what he must do. He must be like the spider and never give up.

He vowed he would be the true king of Scotland or die trying!

Bruce Attacks Scotland

*I*t was not until January 1307 that Robert Bruce finally returned to Scotland. He sent word to the warriors he could still trust to meet him on the island of Arran in western Scotland. They were told to bring their weapons and be ready to invade their own country! The problem was that the Scottish king had been away for such a long time that he didn't know how many English soldiers were in Scotland. Since Bruce only had a small army, before he could attack he needed to know that there were not too many English soldiers. He sent a small group of men onto the Scottish mainland to find out what was going on. The plan was to attack the castle at Turnberry. This was a special place for Bruce because he had been born there. Robert instructed his men to go to the castle and see how many English soldiers were guarding the fortress. If it looked OK to attack, they were to light a bonfire on Turnberry Point. Bruce would see the fire from Arran island and launch his ships.

THE KING SAID BUILD A BONFIRE. HE SAID NOTHING ABOUT FIREWORKS!

Now what happened next is one of those history mysteries. A fire WAS lit on Turnberry Point, but NOT by Bruce's men. Had the English learned about the plan? Were they trying to trick the Scots into attacking a well-defended castle? We will never know. What we do know is that Bruce saw the signal and started the attack. After a year of being invisible, the king of Scotland was once again back on Scottish soil. He must have been a very happy Scot indeed.

It turned out that the castle was heavily guarded by an English knight called Sir Henry Percy and his men. Bruce couldn't risk a direct assault and instead sneakily attacked the nearby village. The English soldiers were all fast asleep. Bruce and his men attacked them before they knew what had hit them — not very fair really. Only one Englishman escaped alive and ran to the castle to tell Percy of the attack. Now Percy was an English knight and was meant to be a bold and brave warrior. So you would expect that on hearing of Bruce outside his castle killing his men, he would pull on his armour, mount his great warhorse and challenge Robert Bruce to a duel — right? Wrong! Percy did the opposite: he hid in his castle and refused to come out and play. Definitely not a Brave Scot!

30

Our hero had learned a very valuable lesson — there were too many English soldiers in Scotland for a battle. So Bruce came up with a plan. He would make it as difficult as possible for the English to stay in Scotland. He would attack them whenever possible, but never fight a big battle. Bruce hoped that the English would just give up and go home.

Oh yeah, one other thing. Bruce had been away for a long time and Edward I was getting old and sick. Everyone knew he didn't have long to live. Now you already know a couple of things about medieval royalty. The first is that when a king died, it was his eldest son who became the next king. The other thing you know is that medieval royal families were rubbish at thinking up names. So it will be no surprise to find out that Edward's son was called — not Robert or Alexander but...you've guessed it... EDWARD. The thing was that the new Edward was a bit of a weakling. In fact he was downright useless and very lazy, definitely not a brave soldier like his father. Robert Bruce knew he would rather fight cowardly King Edward II than his dad.

31

Dead King Edward

King Robert now set about winning back his country. As he marched around Scotland, more and more men came to join him in his fight against the English. Life for the Scottish people under Edward I had been very harsh — in fact it had been downright nasty. The king had made the Scots pay very large taxes and if anyone dared to argue, then he just cut off his head. Chop! Now Edward wasn't all bad! When he caught Robert Bruce's sister, he didn't cut off her head because she was a woman. Instead he thought up a particularly horrible punishment. He placed her in a wooden cage at the top of a tower in Roxburgh Castle and just left her there. Edward had become a very mean old king.

Up until this point Robert's record of fighting battles had been pretty rubbish, but his luck was about to change. He managed to beat the English at Glen Trool and destroyed Aymer de Valence's men at Loudoun Hill, causing the English knight to run for his life. Revenge was sweet for our hero and at last he started to look and act like a true medieval king. The Scottish people

recognised this and began to look on Robert Bruce as their ruler.

On 7th July 1307, everything changed when King Edward I, Longshanks to his enemies, died, aged 69. Edward I had once called himself the Hammer of the Scots and this was true. He was a relentless king, with an ambition to rule Scotland. He had survived rebellions from both William Wallace and Robert Bruce and when he died his armies still controlled much of Scotland. However, his son was a different man. He was not a warrior like his father and definitely not the Hammer of the Scots.

When Edward II became king he was not very bothered about Scotland and even less so about Bruce. This gave King Robert a chance to deal with his Scottish enemies. Bruce had a lot in common with the dead King Edward and had learned how to fight a war. He marched with his army all over Scotland seeking out Scotsmen who didn't think he should be king — don't forget John Balliol was still alive and some people still wanted him back on the throne. Bruce attacked throughout Scotland and won back many castles, eventually beating all of his enemies. The fact that Edward II did not want to fight a war in Scotland meant that Bruce had the time to grow strong. By autumn 1308, King Robert controlled most of Scotland and it was becoming more and more difficult for the new weakling English king to ignore him.

Now you can imagine what Edward I would have done if he had still been alive. He would probably have gathered up all his best knights and marched straight to Scotland to teach our hero a lesson. So, what do you think Edward II did?

Built an army?
Started a war?
Won back Scotland?
No!

Edward II did something his father would never have done. He sent two English knights to arrange a truce with Bruce. This meant both sides agreed not to fight. It lasted until November — the dead king Edward was probably spinning in his grave.

Edward's Army

Once the truce was over Robert Bruce started to attack the English all over again. In fact his men were so successful that the English soldiers were stopped from moving about freely and were forced to stay near the castles and towns they still held. This was mainly in the southeast around Stirling, Edinburgh and Berwick.

RIGHT, YOU TWO GET OUT THERE NOW.

NO WAY! THERE MIGHT BE SCOTS OUT THERE.

Edward II was a weakling king and he had his fair share of problems at home. He had a good friend called Piers Gaveston who was not very popular with the English knights. They thought he was telling the king how to run the country and they were jealous! The knights became so mad that they threatened to start a full-scale war against the king. It was not until 1311 that

Edward was back in full control and could worry about Robert Bruce. He gathered together a large army, and like his daddy had done so many times before, he marched north to fight the Scots.

The army consisted of knights, foot soldiers and archers. To be a knight you needed to have lots of cash and loads of land. They were

mounted on horses that cost a huge amount of money. What made matters worse was that a knight often needed two or three horses, plus servants to look after them all. In fact, most people in medieval England never earned enough money to own a poor old sweaty donkey, never mind a couple of mighty warhorses. As well as the horses, knights needed special armour called chain mail. This was made from lots of rings of steel, welded together to form a coat. On his head a knight wore a metal helmet. As far as weapons were concerned, they fought on the back of their horses using a sword, an axe or even a long spear called a lance. The long and short of it was

knights were big, colourful and very scary!

However, you must remember that knights were only part of the army. The most common type of warrior was called a foot soldier. These men weren't as rich as the knights, but they did have enough money to buy decent armour and weapons. This said, they couldn't afford horses and fought on foot, often carrying a sword, axe or even a long spear. The English army contained lots of foot soldiers and they did most of the fighting. Sometimes, the king used special foot soldiers called mercenaries. These were men from all around the world who would fight for anyone who could pay them.

Knights and foot soldiers were good enough for most generals, but King Edward II had a secret weapon — Welsh longbowmen. His dad had conquered Wales a few years before and now the Welsh were forced to provide long-bowmen for the English army. Longbows were amazing weapons. They stood about six feet high and the men firing the bows needed to be especially strong. In a battle, a bowman fired his arrows high in the air, often shooting them so quickly that four or five were in flight at the same time. The bows were so strong that the arrows could go straight through a wooden door. Can you imagine what would happen if you were hit by one? Splat!

But Bruce was no fool. He knew that the knights and soldiers of the huge English army would need food and wages and that it was the English king who would have to pay them. Bruce decided that if he were able to avoid a big battle, then Edward II would eventually run out of money and have to give up and go home. Surprisingly, this is exactly what happened. Edward II marched into Scotland with his men. Bruce hid and the English left a few months later, with nothing but the possessions they had stolen.

Rope Ladders

With Edward's army gone, Bruce turned his attention to the remaining Scottish castles held by the English. The problem was that Bruce didn't have any of the special weapons he needed to capture the castles. These were called siege engines; they were expensive to make and needed special soldiers to operate them. What Bruce needed was a new way to capture castles. The answer was simple — two ropes, a load of bits of wood and a whole bucketful of luck! Robert Bruce decided that he would use rope ladders to capture the castles. These were special, very light ladders, with a large hook attached to one end. If the hook were thrown against a castle wall, it would stick in the rough stone and the ladder would unroll below it, allowing the soldiers to climb up and over the wall. Bruce planned for the attacks to happen at night and in secret.

The first castle to be attacked was Berwick in 1312. Bruce's men sneaked up to the walls of the town in the dark and threw the rope ladders onto the wall. They started to climb, but they were too noisy and a dog started barking in the town. Soon the English came to see what the problem was and Bruce's men were lucky to escape before they were caught.

By now I am sure you realise that Bruce wasn't the kind of man to just give up. He knew that the rope ladders were a good idea and next decided to attack Perth, but this time he would lead the attack himself. This was very dangerous because if he were caught by the English he would certainly be killed, but he knew it would show his men that he was brave and prepared to die for his country.

Perth was surrounded by a wall and moat. However, the clever Scots knew something the stupid English didn't — the moat wasn't deep enough! Bruce himself led the attack and rushed into the moat. As he waded through the water, it became deeper and deeper, rising first to his waist, then to his chest, before finally stopping at his neck. Bruce and his men were across and the English didn't know a thing about it. They threw their ladders onto the wall and swarmed up and over. The English soldiers in Perth were so surprised by Bruce's attack that they surrendered without a fight. The rope ladders had worked!

In February 1314 Bruce turned his attention to Roxburgh Castle. This time he instructed James Douglas to attack with the rope ladders.

I DON'T THINK THE ROPE LADDER IDEA IS THAT GOOD AFTER ALL.

Douglas
and his men
crept up to the walls
of the castle without being seen.
They used the rope ladders to scale
the wall and once inside, the castle
was quickly taken and then burned
to the ground.

Edinburgh Castle was next. On
14th March, Bruce told Thomas
Randolph to attack the castle.
It is likely that the soldiers were
expecting the attack and were on
the lookout for intruders carrying
rope ladders. So Randolph tried
something a bit different.
Edinburgh Castle was built on the
top of a huge rock with only one
way in. He sent most of his men to
the door at the front of
the castle. The English saw
them coming and rushed to
defend the gates.

This was just what Randolph
wanted. Whilst his men were
knocking on the front door, he
was going to get in around the
back. He gathered his small group
of men and, armed with rope
ladders, swarmed up the cliff
below the walls. Then they threw
up the ladders and climbed the
walls, quickly killing the
unsuspecting guards and opening
the front gate to let in the rest of
the army. Once inside, the castle
was quickly taken and burned to
the ground so the English couldn't
use it.

Bruce's Favourite Axe

*D*espite the Scottish success in winning back their castles, one stronghold remained in English hands — Stirling Castle. It was perched high on a craggy rock and could only be attacked from one side. Edward Bruce, the king's brother, was given the difficult job of capturing this castle. The English all now knew about the rope ladder trick and it wasn't going to work again. Edward had no choice but to surround the castle and try to starve the English out. He placed his men in a big circle and waited and waited and waited and waited. In the end he began to realise that the castle would not be captured in this way.

Edward Bruce now tried a new approach and asked the English if they would give up. They weren't stupid, but they knew that the only chance they had to escape was rescue by another English army. They told Edward Bruce that if, in one year's time, King Edward II had not come to help them, then they would give up the castle without a fight.

IF YOU COME OUT NOW, I WILL BE YOUR BEST FRIEND.

NO AND GO AWAY. YOUR ARMY IS SPOILING THE NICE VIEW.

Edward Bruce agreed to this, but without consulting his brother. When Robert Bruce found out what his brother had done, he was hopping mad. Our hero knew that the English king wouldn't be able to ignore this challenge and would have no choice but to bring an army to Scotland. Robert Bruce would have to do the one thing he had avoided for all those years — fight the English in a big battle.

Soon, Edward II was ready to march into Scotland to rescue the English from Stirling castle. He had gathered together about 15,000 foot soldiers and 2,500 knights. However, Robert knew all about the English plans and had also called his men to fight. The Scottish army was different to the English and was made up of about 5,000 foot soldiers, armed with long spears. They also had about 500 horsemen, but these were no match for the mighty English knights.

The English army moved to Edinburgh and then onward to Falkirk. As the English army came closer to Stirling, Robert Bruce gathered his men together in an area a few miles south of the castle. Bruce positioned his men on high ground with their backs to some woods and with

YOUR MAJESTY, YOUR ARMY IS WAITING FOR ITS ORDERS.

CAN'T YOU SEE I AM BUSY?

the Bannock Burn, a large stream, running in front of them.

On the morning of Sunday 23rd June, the English advanced along the Edinburgh–Stirling road, just south of the Scots. Useless Edward II was already having difficulty controlling his army and failed to give his men clear orders. So as they advanced they simply didn't know what their king wanted them to do. When word reached the English knights that the Scots were only a few miles away, they started to make up their own plans. They decided that they wanted to get at the Scottish as soon as possible and raced ahead, alone, without the support of any foot soldiers or archers.

The English knights quickly came to the bottom of a hill with a large wood at the top. The main part of the Scottish army was hiding in the woods and the English knights could only see a handful of Scottish horsemen on the hill. Unable to resist the chance to kill a few Scots, one young knight broke away and charged forward. His name was Sir Henry de Bohun

crown. It was Robert Bruce, alone and unguarded. Henry de Bohun thundered on, lowering his lance, coming closer and closer to the Scottish king. Yet the Brave Scot didn't move, he just stayed still on his horse, watching the deadly knight. Just as the two men were about to meet and the English lance was going to plunge into Bruce's heart, he moved. He pulled hard on the reins of his horse, dragging it to one side and avoiding the deadly lance. As the weapon rushed harmlessly past the king, the Englishmen knew he was in trouble. He was unable to stop his horse. As he rode next to Bruce, the king acted. He stood tall in his stirrups and swung his axe high into the air, bringing it down onto the knight's helmet. The blow was truly mighty. It struck Sir Henry so hard that it broke his helmet and split his head clean in two!

and as he thundered up the hill he saw something that made his eyes jump out of their sockets. In front of him was a Scottish warrior, mounted on a horse, dressed in chain mail armour and carrying just an axe. On top of his metal helmet was secured a bright silver

As the axe met with
bone and brain, it shattered
and the handle split. The
Englishmen's lifeless body fell
bloodily from the horse and
the king of Scotland was safe.

As he rode back to his army they cheered and yelled, but the Scottish knights were angry. Bruce had risked his life. They shouted at the king for taking such a mad risk. Robert ignored them; instead he simply commented that he was very sad that he had broken his favourite axe on the head of a stupid English knight.

The story of the Brave Scot spread quickly through the ranks of the Scottish army, and within a few hours every man was talking of the duel. Bruce's gamble had worked. Bruce was now a legend and his men were prepared to die for such a brave leader.

Yet the day's fighting was not over. Behind Sir Henry's dead body a force of bloodthirsty English knights had formed to take his place. They charged up the hill and the Scottish warriors emerged from the woods to meet them. The fighting was fierce and much blood was spilled. Eventually the English had to withdraw, since they had no foot soldiers or bowmen to help with the battle. It was getting dark and the fight would have to wait until the next day.

IT WAS MY FAVOURITE AXE.

Bannockburn

During the night, Robert Bruce thought seriously about retreating and avoiding battle. However, after speaking to his knights, he decided that if they were to beat the English in battle, this would be the best chance they would ever get.

As the next day dawned, the Scots were ready for battle. In the early morning sun, they advanced out of the woods to face the English who had drawn up their soldiers at the foot of the hill. During the night, the English had crossed the Bannock Burn and now stood with it close behind them — a move many of the soldiers wouldn't live to regret. The Scottish foot soldiers were in a special formation called a schiltrom, which William Wallace had taught them. The men were organised into small groups and armed with very long spears. They arranged themselves so the spears stuck out in all directions — a bit like a hedgehog. The warriors at the front knelt on the floor and the men behind pushed their spears over the front rank's shoulders.

They had practised and practised forming into the schiltrom until they could do it perfectly.

As King Edward II looked on, he could not believe what he was seeing. He really thought that the Scottish army would not be stupid enough to fight his mighty English soldiers. So, when the Scots stopped marching and dropped to their knees to pray, Edward was confused. He laughed and turned to his men saying, "Look, they pray for my mercy."

One of Edward's knights replied, "They do ask for mercy my Lord, but not from you, from God." It must have been the first time Edward was really scared of the Scots.

The battle opened with a brief exchange of arrows, followed by the first charge from the English knights. They smashed into the leading schiltrom, but the hedge of spears did its job and many of the knights were killed. The rest of the schiltroms now did something that had never been seen before — ever. The spearmen attacked the knights! Staying in one big mass they pushed onto the horses, killing them where they stood. The knights were all squashed together and pushed down the hill. With the river right behind them, the horseman had nowhere to escape — they stood no chance against the

solid spears. Slowly, as the king watched, hundreds of English knights and noblemen were squashed together and killed by the Scots.

Finally, the king reacted and brought into the battle the dreaded longbowmen. These could fire arrows into the schiltroms, killing the Scots without fear of being hurt. However, the stupid king had even managed to get this wrong. During the panic of the battle, the longbowmen had become spread out all over the battlefield. The king could only gather together a small group of archers. As if this were not bad enough for the English king, Robert Bruce was just about to make matters worse. Since all the English knights were busy fighting for their lives against the schiltroms, the Scottish king was free to order his small group of horsemen to attack. They rushed down the hillside, into the sorry mass of Welsh longbowmen. The poor archers were swept away.

What remained of the English foot soldiers now sprinted forward to join the battle. However, they had very little room, and eager to get involved in the fight, they pushed up against the back of the knights. The Scots responded quickly and sent what was left of their foot soldiers into the deadly mass of swords and spears.

The fighting had turned into a huge disorganised mêlée, with each man fighting for his life.